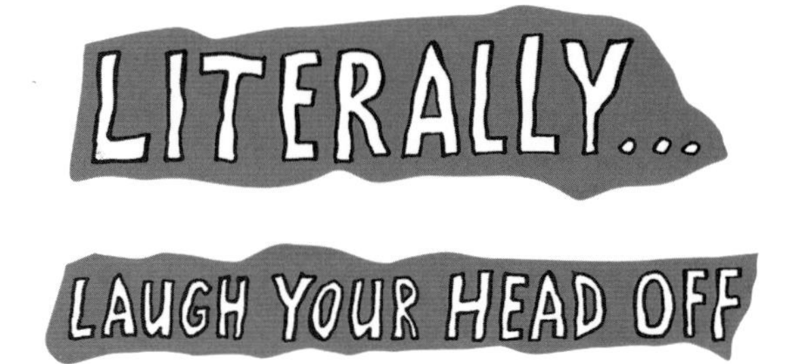
LITERALLY...
LAUGH YOUR HEAD OFF

HA HA HA HA

PRION

With thanks to Pete Bishop and
Nicola Sherring for helpful thoughts

First published in Great Britain in 2007 by

Prion
an imprint of the
Carlton Publishing Group
20 Mortimer Street
London W1T 3JW

2 4 6 8 10 9 7 5 3 1

A catalogue record for this book is available from the British Library

ISBN 978-1-85375-636-8

Printed and bound in Singapore

For my children – all five

Foreword

For years I have been hoping that Steven Appleby might be moved to illustrate a book on this topic ... and now he has done it.

I am literally thrilled to bits.

P.P.
Editorial Director
Prion

May 2007

"TLC literally exploded onto the music scene in 1992 with their debut album, *Ooooooh!*"

— *The Inside Connection* magazine

Here we come!
BA BA BOOM!

"Space-station Mir is literally a few tin cans joined together"

— Space correspondent, BBC Radio Five Live

I expected it to be bigger.

"The BBC has literally wiped the floor with the opposition"

— Lord Peston, Select Committee on BBC Charter Review,
Minutes of Evidence, 20 July 2005

"Two Mafia bosses escaped from a courthouse literally from under the noses of their guards"

— BBC Radio 4

Aah... Aah...
Aah...

"Drogba literally destroyed Senderos today"

— Former footballer Jamie Redknapp
on the Carling Cup final,
25 February 2007

Bit of a rough tackle there...
Yesiree, Bob.
PETROL
GAS
WOOD
FEET
GO NOWHER

"Going for a higher, more desolate sound, frontman and slide player Jeffrey Lee Pierce and his band were literally on fire"

— Thom Jurek, All Music Guide
online review of Miami's album
The Gun Club, December 2006

We're standing by. Sounds good!
Hose me! Hose me!

"The ball was literally glued to the back of his foot – into the back of the net"

— Sports commentator Alan Parry

“I know there are many people who are literally quaking in their boots”

— Author Mark Lynas in a discussion
about climate change,
Today, BBC Radio 4,
20 April 2007

Waaa... I'm quaking in my boots!
Actually, those are MY boots!
And YOU'RE quaking in MY slippers...
QUAKING IN HER STOCKING FEET

"It literally strikes a chord in people's hearts"

— Michael Parkinson on Tony Bennett's performance
of the song "I Left My Heart in San Francisco",
Parkinson, Channel 4 TV,
4 November 2006

a
?
b

c
Scalpel...
Tuning fork...

"Britain is literally turning into a nation of couch potatoes"

— Comment on rising obesity rates,
Today, BBC Radio 4

“One lady was literally beside herself with rage, pointing out that this was because we’d spent trillions of dollars to repair Iraq’s infrastructure and this was just our come-uppin’s [*sic*] for that kind of irresponsibility”

— Jim W. Coleman, online report on the 2006
Hanukkah Eve windstorm “After the Storm”,
December 2006

I'm beside myself!
Me too!
And me!
I'm behind myself.

“In the regiments of the United States Colored Troops, to which he had literally given birth, there was no doubt Lincoln sat at the head of the table”

— From *Lincoln’s Men: How President Lincoln Became Father to an Army and a Nation*, by William C. Davis, 2000

“As soon as I looked at the children I could tell ... it was 95 degrees and they were literally baking”

— Sheriff Fred Abdalla, Jefferson County, Colorado, USA,
after arresting a woman for having sunburnt children,
August 2002

Sniff sniff... Nearly done.

“James Milner is literally hugging the touchline”

— Football correspondent,
BBC Radio Five Live

"So you drink mineral drinks and carbohydrate drinks, and are quite literally bursting for a pee by the time you get to the car. That's why you see drivers jumping over the wall at the start of a race. Actually, I think it sharpens you up"

— Racing driver Damon Hill,
The Independent, March 1998

Aaaah...
The relief!

"The taxi is tiny – I'm literally shoe-horned into the front seat"

— Report on Beijing, BBC Radio Five Live,
1 February 2002

SELF-DRIVE

“We have literally barrow-loads of evidence that cigarette advertising does not increase smoking habits”

— Max Mosley, BBC Radio Five Live

ADVERTISEMENT
COLLECT
10,000 BUTTS
AND WE'LL GIVE YOU...
A PACK OF CIGGIES!
CAN'T SAY FAIRER THAN THAT, EH?
HAPPY SMOKING!
MANLEY'S
20
NO
DIE, SCUM!

“I saw journalists become animals, literally”

— US politician Gary Hart in 1998,
recalling the reporting frenzy that put paid to his US
Presidential prospects when his sexual peccadilloes
were exposed in 1987

“The village has literally been through a mangle”

— News reporter Bob Sinkinson,
BBC Radio Five Live

Hurry up, dear, there are loads more villages over here.
There goes our house!

“All hell broke loose – literally”

— Report on the rowdy Lewis–Tyson press conference,
BBC Radio Five Live, June 2002

Damnation!
Yes.
It must be something you said!

"History is literally unfolding in front of your eyes"

— Caroline Hawley, BBC correspondent in Baghdad,
April 2003

It's never as easy to fold it up again.

"I literally devoured this book. In about 16 or 17 hours I had finished it cover to cover"

— Simon Cleveland, USA, Amazon online review of Robert Kurson's *Shadow Divers*, 1 June 2006

GRUNT
GUZZLE
LADY-LIKE
DUNKING
DAINTY
LADIES

"Students at the University of Warwick are almost literally burning the midnight oil; they have persuaded the University to keep its library open for reference and private study from 9.30pm to midnight each weekday night during term"

— University of Warwick press release,
25 March 1999

Don't be silly, it's just CALLED midnight oil. We'll burn it at lunchtime.
MIDNIGHT OIL

"The swifts were literally hoovering up the flies"

— Ornithologist and presenter Bill Oddie,
BBC2 TV

Get the oven on, Mrs Swift. Flies for supper tonight.
Ok love.
Yow!
Help!
Yike!
Whoooooo...

“This is in no way your average, everyday Hummer H3. This baby literally has all the bells and whistles!!”

— EBay online car advertisement,
April 2007

IF YOU WANT A CAR WITH BELLS AND WHISTLES THEN THIS BEAUTY IS FOR YOU!

"This quote from [the novel] *What's a Girl Gotta Do?* was one that had me literally cracking up with laughter"

— Eileen Famiglietti, Massachusetts, USA,
Amazon online review,
30 January 2003

You need to start using a moisturiser.

"The players literally only have to fall out of their beds to be on the training pitch"

— Dunfermline football manager
Jimmy Calderwood

Darling?
Pity it's such a long fall!

“India will quite literally be your oyster”

— Advertisement for an Indian cooking holiday,
onthegotours.com

Aargh!
Adaii!
Help!

A search party was "literally heading for a cross on a map"

— *The Guardian*, September 2000

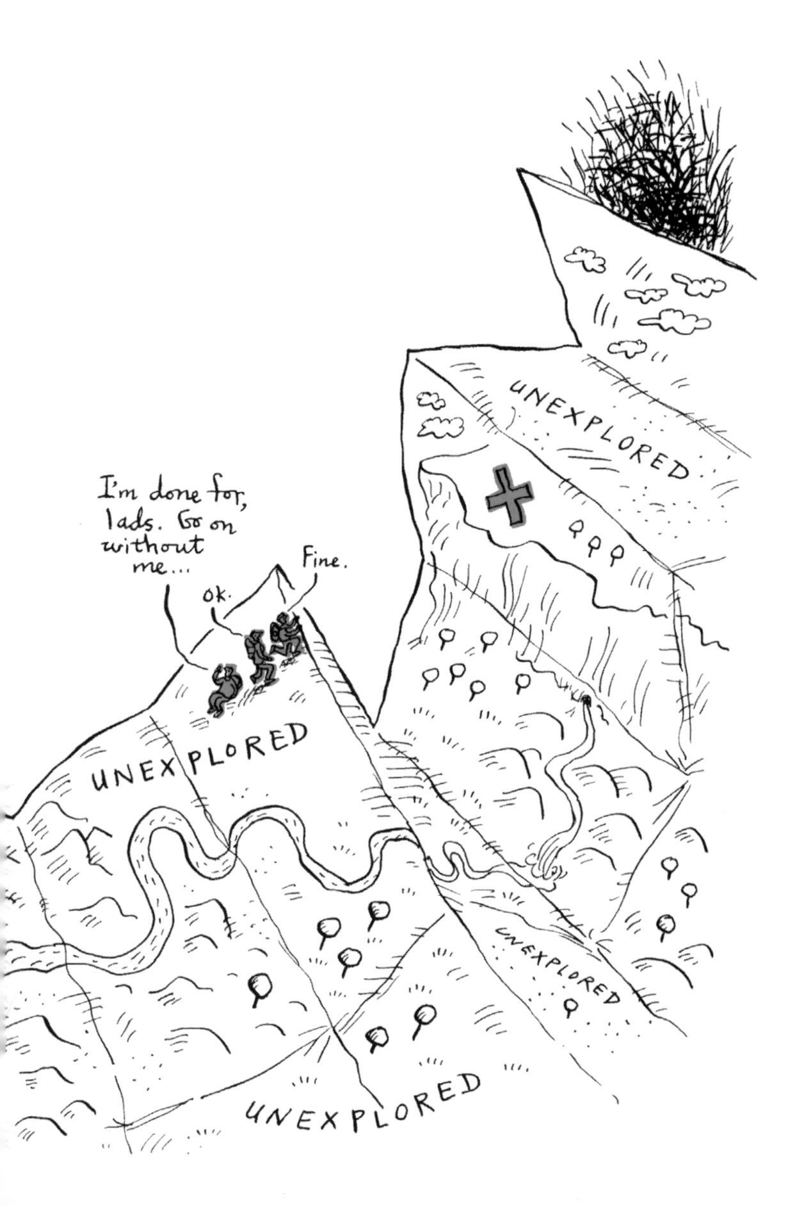
I'm done for, lads. Go on without me...
Ok.
Fine.
UNEXPLORED
UNEXPLORED
UNEXPLORED
UNEXPLORED
UNEXPLORED

"As athletes these triple jumpers are literally human kangaroos"

— Stuart Storey, commentating on the 2006 European Athletics Championships, BBC TV

SPROING!
Well, they're disqualified, then.

“When Andre Agassi meets a qualifier, he tends to literally steamroller them”

— Tennis correspondent Ian Carter,
BBC Radio Five Live

HE'S disqualified, too!

“Michael Jackson almost literally stole the headlines”

— Channel 4 TV *News*

Michael Jackson has been cutting up my paper... AGAIN!

"Trains are running 25 per cent slower
because the tracks are literally cooking"

— *Newsbeat*, BBC Radio 1

Crunchy.
This is your train manager... We apologise for the slight delay to your service today...

"The police were literally swimming in a sea of red herrings"

— *Sun* reporter on the Jill Dando murder trial, January 2003

POLICE

"Heath Ledger's literally monumental performance in *Brokeback* is a study in chipped granite that revises American masculinity as surely as Brando or Elliott Gould"

— From the seventh annual
Village Voice film critics' poll,
December 2005

Congratulations. You've got the part.

"Vieira was robbed by Pires, quite literally"

— Clive Tyldesley, commentating on the
Arsenal v Juventus game in the
Champions League 2006, ITV

Keep the ball. I'm off to sell this lot.
Disqualified!
THE SHIRT OFF HIS BACK

“There aren’t many Page 3 girls – literally a handful”

— Disc jockey Chris Moyles,
– BBC Radio 1

Their breasts look bigger in photos
So do they.

"Before Senator Sam Ervin's Committee, Dean's testimony was electrifying – he literally spilled the beans on the Nixon Administration, from which they were never able to recover"

— Mobiusein, retrospective comment on the
US Watergate scandal, dailykos.com,
22 March 2007

BEST
QUALITY
BEANS
oops

“This chilli will literally blow your head off!”

— UKTV Food Channel

BLAM!

"Writing in the *Sunday Times* [of India] (26 August, 1990) Mahaweli Development Ministry Official Herman Gunaratne literally let the cat out of the bag when he confessed, *inter alia*, thus: 'All wars are fought for land ... ' "

— V. Thangavelu, online report
"Sinhalese Have Cause to Celebrate the Golden Jubilee of Gal Oya Colonization Scheme"

Right, it's time for a few home truths! Lucky I'm a talking cat...

The world had “literally gone pear-shaped”

— *The Guardian*,
September 2000

And we all know how quickly pears go mushy.
Ugh. I've stood in a rotten bit.

"The 9/11 threat literally froze the passengers of a Hyderabad-bound train following a bomb hoax call"

— *The Times of India*

EAT

"Kelly [Sotherton] has the whole crowd here and literally running the 800 metres with her"

— Former athlete Colin Jackson,
commentating on the European Indoor Athletics
Championships in Birmingham,
BBC2 TV, March 2007

I've no option but to disqualify you ALL!

“We’ve literally head-hunted the best group of buyers in the business”

— QVC Shopping Channel

We're head-hunted the very best...
And now WE'RE the best!

"They have literally ploughed millions of pounds into the town's hospital"

— Wyre Borough Council press release,
February 2003

They're ruined the corridors!
Should have spent the money on equipment.
oops!

"A tripod system is literally an extension of a cameraman's limb on the field"

— Panther Film Equipment promotion,
November 2005

“The viewer literally becomes a meerkat”

— *Mischievous Meerkats*,
TV Discovery Channel

Damn these paws!

"I was really excited that I went ahead to play Hobart because I was really rusty, and I can see the rust shedding from my game literally"

— Professional tennis player
Serena Williams, January 2007

POK!
Aah. Rust in my eye!

“We literally jumped on a plane to Beijing”

— Athlete Darren Campbell talking to Gary Richardson,
Today, BBC Radio 4,
15 August 2006

Excuse me...
Excuse me...

"I was literally hung out to dry by Tony Blair and his government"

— Des Smith, teacher and former adviser to Blair's Special Schools and Academies Trust, interviewed by the *News of the World*, 18 February 2007

They put me in the spin-dryer first, then through the mangle...
AND I've shrunk!

“To me, taking James Bond back to the basics – literally, back to square one – might have seemed a daunting task”

— Jenny J.J.I., Florida, USA,
Amazon online review of the film *Casino Royale*,
17 April 2007

Now that you have regressed to square one you are doomed, Mr Bond!
Ga.*

* Bugger.

“When I first walked into the marvellous creation that is the opera house built for *Phantom* in the Venetian, I was literally gobsmacked”

— Composer Andrew Lloyd Webber,
describing the set of *Phantom of the Opera* in Las Vegas,
from the souvenir programme

I'll teach you to talk out of your bottom!
YOW! OUCH!

"Despite the literally gut-wrenching manner in which Tottenham lost their Champions League spot to Arsenal ... "

— Ray Collins on the 2005/06 football season,
The Sunday Telegraph,
22 October 2006

Oh no - they're using a gut-wrenching machine!

"They [the supermarkets] can literally play God, even to the point of sending food back to the genetic drawing board for a redesign"

— *The Guardian*, 1995

ARCHANGEL TESCO AND ARCHANGEL ASDA AMUSE THEMSELVES BY DESTROYING CORNER SHOPS.

"[Farmers are] literally tearing their hair out trying to make a living"

— Edward Leigh talking to Edward Stourton,
Today, BBC Radio 4, 18 October 2006

THE BIG BAG OF ORGANIC
FARMER'S HAIR
INSTRUCTIONS: SOW IN ROWS. DO NOT THIN OUT.
BEFORE ~
AFTER ~
COLOUR:
GREY

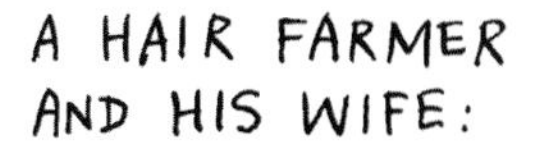
A HAIR FARMER
AND HIS WIFE:

“That was hit with such power it’s literally gone through Michael Clarke at gully”

— Former cricketer Michael Slater on the
2005 Ashes series, Channel 4 TV

“People have literally voted with their feet”

— Review of the Great North Run,
BBC Radio Five Live

Yuk. Can I have a different pencil, please?

“People will risk life and limb darting in and out of traffic on foot to get a glimpse of Michael [Jackson] or to touch him. The fans in Japan literally inhale him ... ”

— *Chicago Sun Times*, March 2007

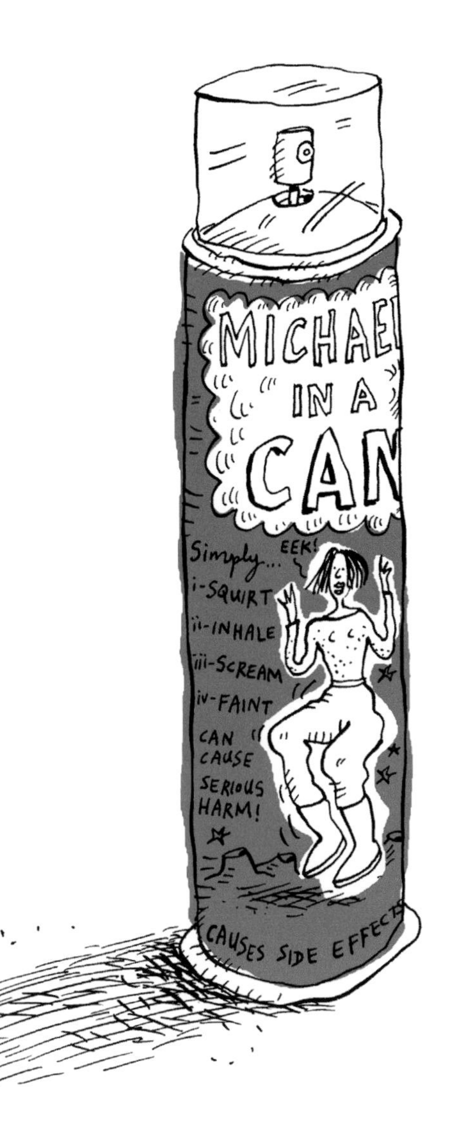
MICHAEL
IN A
CAN
Simply...
EEK!
i-SQUIRT
ii-INHALE
iii-SCREAM
iv-FAINT
CAN CAUSE SERIOUS HARM!
CAUSES SIDE EFFECTS

"Alzheimer's is a cruel disease; it causes someone to literally disintegrate before your very eyes"

— BBC News 24

Dad thinks we're all aboard the starship Enterprise.
Beam me up!
Wheee!
Beep beep!

“As the seconds tick down, Belgium are literally playing in time that doesn’t exist”

— ITV commentator Guy Mowbray

But we scored 3 goals!
Sorry. That time didn't exist.
Aw, ref!

"Joanna Lumley has long been known for a series of roles in film and television which have literally jumped out of the screen"

— Presenter Jenni Murray, *Woman's Hour*,
BBC Radio 4, 23 March 2007

Gotcha!

“Quite literally, you would not have put your shirt on him two weeks ago”

— Sports commentator Clive Tyldesley

Obviously I wouldn't put MY shirt on him... So I gave him yours. And your shoes.

“He has literally put his money where his mouth is”

— Comment on the new British Telecom Chairman
Christopher Bland, BBC Radio Five Live,
May 2001

Hang on while I find my wallet...
RUMMAGE
No thanks, Guv. This one's on me
TAXI

"Roy Keane has got too big for his boots, literally"

— Football commentator Mike Ingham,
BBC Radio Five Live

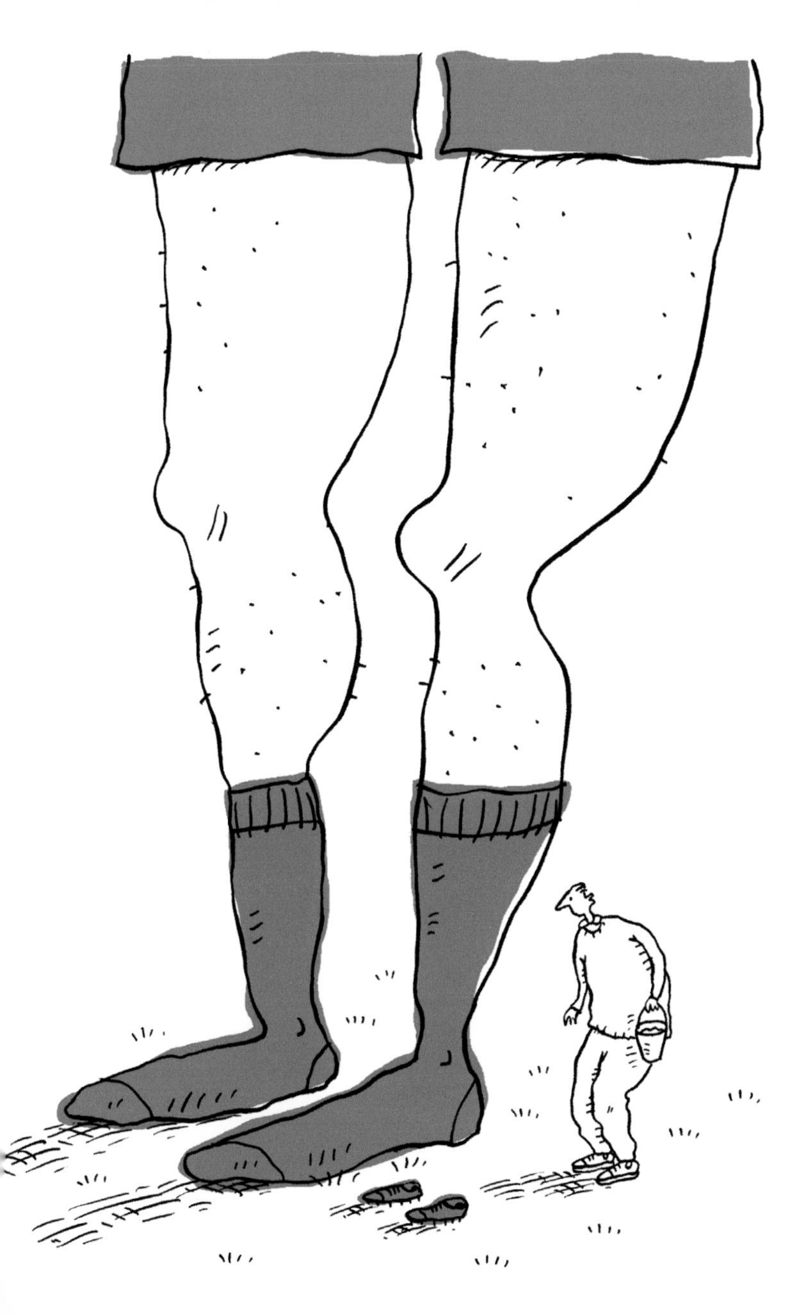

"Following Hurricane Mitch, food supplies in Honduras have literally been running out"

— BBC Radio 4, October 1998

Now that I've seen your eyes and teeth I've lost my appetite.

"Literally virtually 800 metres from the seafront"

— Brighton estate agent information,
March 2003

And can you see the sea?
With my X-ray vision, yes.
ESTATE AGENT
DETAILS

"What was it like when literally the whole world stopped to notice you?"

— Presenter John Inverdale,
On Side, BBC1 TV

"I fell off the plank because, literally, my legs went to jelly"

— TV presenter Davina McCall,
Zoe Ball Breakfast Show,
BBC Radio 1

SHRIEK!
my legs have turned
fat and purple!

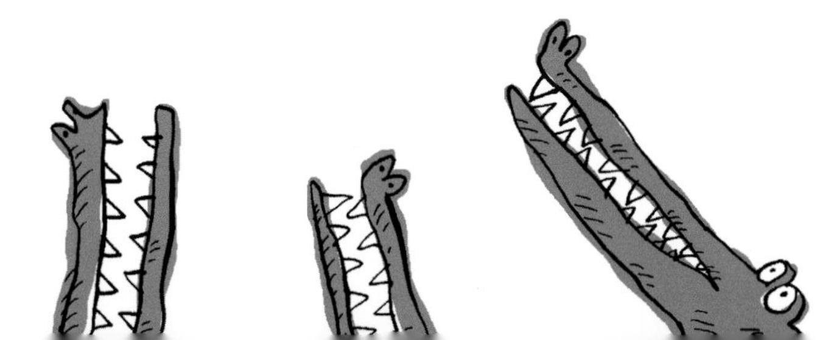

"When I downloaded this game and my trial was over, I ran over to my husband and literally cried my eyes out begging him to buy the game for me!"

— Yahoo! Games online user review of Diner Dash,
29 November 2005

Waaaaaa...

"Cristiano Ronaldo goes down far too easily for my liking, but remember he's literally had two big men up his backside for 90 minutes"

— Tony Gale on Sky Sports, as reported in
Zoo Weekly magazine, 23–29 March 2007

Hey!
Get up!
Chop chop!
Come on, asshole!
SLAP!

"I am *not exaggerating* – my child is literally coughing his head off"

— Message on paedatrician's answering machine,
reported on literally.barelyfitz.com,
25 February 2006

Cover your mouth, Duncan!
COUGH COUGH COUGH COUGH COUGH COUGH
Sorry, Mum.
COUGH COUGH COUGH COUGH COUGH COUGH COUGH COUGH COUGH COUGH COUGH COUGH

"Liverpool have literally come back from the grave"

— Report on Liverpool's comeback in
the UEFA Champions League Final,
BBC sports news, May 2005

To me!

"This was literally a shocking murder"

— *Newsnight*, BBC2 TV

“ ‘One of the symptoms of food allergy is dread,’ Mindlin explains. ‘She knows something is very wrong and literally tries to jump out of her skin. It’s unbearable to watch.’ ”

— Pamela Paul, “Allergies at the Dinner Table”,
time.com, 22 November 2006

Surprise!
Hey! You're jumped out of someone else's skin.

"I must point out that I was literally dying of laughter throughout and hence did not make an objective report of events"

— Ravi Mantha, online review of an evening at the Nehru Centre

Not long now. He's having the last laugh.
HAW HAW HAW HAW HAW HAW HAW HAW HAW HAW HAW HAW HAW HAW...

"Phew. Finished at last. I'm literally so dog-tired I think I'll just close my eyes for a moment ... "

— Steven Appleby, 31 May 2007

ZZZZZZ